CW00551991

SKINLESS 👓

COLETTE SENSIER

SKINLESS

 EYEWEAR PUBLISHING

First published in 2014
by Eyewear Publishing Ltd
74 Leith Mansions, Grantully Road
London w9 1lJ
United Kingdom

Typeset with graphic design by Edwin Smet
Printed in England by TJ International Ltd, Padstow, Cornwall

WWW.EYEWEARPUBLISHING.COM

Colette Sensier was born in Brighton in 1988, and now lives and works in London. She studied English at Kings' College, Cambridge, lived for short periods in Crete and Bulgaria, and graduated from UEA with an MA in Creative Writing (Prose). Colette's work has featured in Oxfam's *Asking a Shadow to Dance*, New Writing South's *Poetry South East 2010*, Salt's *Best British Poetry 2011*, the *Salt Book of Younger Poets* and Eyewear's *Lung Jazz*, as well as various magazines. Her debut pamphlet, *How Many Camels Is Too Many?*, was published by Holdfire Press in 2012.

Table of Contents

Total Resurrection of the Body

My grandfather believed
in total resurrection of the body.
He'd watch my fingernails
drop into the washbasin,

torn between my father's teeth
when I was a baby; later,
sunk in the depths of carpet
underneath my bed.

Each time he cut my hair
a little more of my mortality
slipped down my back into the world.
It didn't matter. No need even

for organs to stay put,
they were free to fly
out of broken skin; blood
replenishable with pints hanging in bags

at the cosmic butchers.
My liver, kidneys, heart
could be called back like dogs.
He didn't doubt his original hip

would come running at the final call,
that last light, when his family
will gather round his bed,
and a life's worth of fingernails

follow in his slipstream
up to Heaven, and coat him
like feathers on an Aztec eagle
as he sits at God's intact right hand.

DNA

I imagine he could really track it down,
a single pale cell on a glass tray
glowing like a lightbulb's skin.

Imagine that he knows what he's looking at:
the almost invisible thing
which makes all the difference.
The scientist gulps with excitement.

His breath shakes the cell,
a tremor like the eye's leap behind the lid,
one thousand times reduced.
Stop. He exhales relief,

looks down – and the tray's empty;
the spine of matter flexed and gone,
its flutter stilled by the heavy living breeze.

I Have My Mother's Eyes

Since the laser sliced through a small part of my inheritance,
I see your face correctly, as it is,
but the restaurant's hollow heat is too much
for my new tear ducts. They itch at particles of light,

at pieces of our skins, the shellfish and the bowls they're served in.
Your eyes make coracles for their waste dust,
loose pearls sheening the jelly screen
behind the eyelid. Mine are bent locks, stuttering

tears back down the gullet of an unknown passage
to a place as strange, as old, as another species' heart and lungs.
I know from when they touched me, anaesthetised,
that eyes are eyeless, nerveless, senseless; like the mussels

flexing below me in their cool broth: breathless fish surprised
when I prise them from the crafts they cling to;
shells that once clung to open-handed waves.
There's no telling whether their slack ovals

are one with the calf-curved shells, or just their tenants;
no way to tell the skulker from the skull. You'll only find out when
you break the root keeping them in touch –
when you listen with another sense,

for the high-pitched tear wrenched
from something nearly inanimate...
                                        Across the table,
you throw back your head and down your oyster
in a one-way liquid gulp.

Recapitulation Theory

First the round cheek of the taut stomach,
navel an ear or blowhole, listening out
for signals from the curved inverted globe.
Then the bones, once out, moulding their sphere.

The halfway house retreats. Darkened eyelashes
frame new eyes; the layer of thin dried yoghurt
flakes away. Coarse hair falls from his cheeks
in the slow move from prehistory to now,

a gill-less creature. Or, as it goes for me:
the face smooths itself out as I recline,
Madonna of the incidental, waiting
for the roots of things to show. I listen to lost notes,

the silent progress of the gut-shot features
swimming back to their original element.

Song of Zagreus

Zagreus dances
all around the circle of the moon,
his hands on his hips,

his squashed boy's face
gurning in the lilywhite night.

He changes colour
like a strip of bronze dangling
before a fire.

Morning comes
and Zagreus hides in the jungle,
his eyes skipping
through the leaves and bushes.

His rabbit-paw fist is missing.
His slender foot is still tapping.

Zagreus looks at me through the blue sea,
and his skin slips from him,
like the skein of salt glitter
cast on midday water,

like blood separating itself from oil
to float crimson to the top of the jar —

      and then he's gone.

There is almost no noise.

I pick up Zagreus' elbow like a knuckle of meat
and bring it to my mouth.

It smells like

★

stones and bottles left to clash
in the park,

smells like

an orgy of skin become grey dust
on a white glove,

smells like

rain on bracken and earth

★

like

the shadows floating in the moon's perfect circle,
things whose hands touch their own toes.

Praise for a Recovering Doctor

When you pick up the scalpel and hold it like something electric,
known space spreading up the nerves from air to brain-twitch;
and your other hand moves like Braille across the draped body,

making sense of patterns like train-tracks, a skin-layer away,
I want to praise you with all my words, right down
to the pills clustered at the bottom of your handbag, the three

espressos on your breath. I'll praise your feet on the ground,
your labcoat and the skin you tear like cloud or linked neurons;
like what it is. You put down the knife and turn to me

and smile like a jeweller who's spent hours
with a wet cloth, shining a sapphire, till his reflection
is held firm in a square of touchable light. I remember that dark day

when you rocked on the floor, and your heart and liver shook,
naked in the face of god. Now, when you remove
the cold brown meat from others, I swear I see them pulse.

Refugees

This is where they are now, the adored.
This is where they are: they are transferred.
They are blinks, the gaps at midnight.

They ride for miles covered in damp sand:
old, or else bleeding; shoddy or else naked.
They are next to you but on a different continent;

they are wonderful and you have to laugh.
They carry the love they once had on top of their skin,
like salt worn in by rough, uncultivated fingers,
lines of gold carelessly mined.

I'll see you back at that same place,
as we construct it like a tent, and save ourselves,
tipping our chairlegs towards each other,
sweeping a third round across the table.

We'll watch the other chosen people move
against each other, across the printed carpet.
Watch dents left where their own countries –

discovered with a blessing and a prayer,
made up on maps and marked –
have left them, calling to be followed.

Orpheus

i.

After I'd hustled, somehow, my way through overdrafts and overtime,
goat-sitting, busking on street corners – I drew quite a crowd – into
the trans-continental-ticket bracket, packed my handbooks and mosquito nets,
boarded at the Styx and sung the long ripped song of the aeroplane,

a birdcall lost in chasing cloud, I landed slap-bang in the middle of *Mahebourg Market,*
Mauritius, the place I'd hoped to seek her out: my other half, my home;
the wandering, trapped part of my soul I'd been promised I could always
return to. I staggered when I got there though, under the weight of clatter

and the strange stray dogs, and white wolves of waves stroking the surfaces
of a landscape burnt too hot for me. And I despaired, the thing that I most wanted
nowhere to be found among t-shirts imported from Japan, clacking boules,
the bang of stacked chapatti pans, and the gasps of local magicians

astonished at themselves and all they had to offer. Was that her eye in the eye
of a fat round fish flapping at the top of a silvery pile, sounding the echo
of a sunbeam? Was that her body turning in the pink jewelled sari
held up for admiration, moving like mobile hair or flayed skin? The imam

called over my head, *remember to submit*. The church bells told me, *come back*
to God. Salt scent whispered behind lashes and fingernails, weaving across the veins
at my wrists. The lute bumped against the suddenly wrong skin of my thigh,
a skin too pale and too loosely held to bone, as I dodged from toe to toe and string

to string around the docks, never fast enough to catch a single sincere note;
as policemen with their bushed moustaches, blue shirts and sunglassed eyes watched me
like deaf spirits, separated tourists who dared to kiss. *Is this, sir,*
what you're looking for? Peek quickly or they'll kick me out, he opened up

the long flat hook of his grey suitcase,
the lid swung up like the stone before a tomb...

ii.

Many words have been suggested to or given me:
Greek or Turkish? Italiano, Español? There's no way
you're not Israeli or *Where was your mother from?*
At most, *You have the island look. Caribbean?*
but here they speak to me in Kreol, watch me

as I walk down the street – until I answer
and, as always, disappoint; my staccato English
failed again. So my mouth stays folded up.
I watch my grandparents instead
as they lie on tender beaches, remembering;

or else I watch the people as they move
from one palm to the next, their faces
heavy in the shade – reflecting, like thick glass
tilted towards the sun, nothing but the island's
hot light. Nothing of me.

iii.

It's not many human creatures who – with skin
living and flexible working over solid limbs
full of dry, shining, salted bone,
a purple pumping heart, kidneys and lungs –
will know the feeling of complete immersion,
the journey to another land behind a wall of salt
and glass and water. It's not many who cross
that floating river, spitting pomegranate seeds,
and live to tell the tale.

But when you dived off that ledge or throne of rock
and felt the water popping in your ears,
scouring your throat to take what it discovered there,
peeling the layer of skin around your lips,
you knew you had become mankind, and knew
what you had found – a story that would save us all,
the hint of an ending in eighteen feet of water,
a glimpse of Eurydice.

And then the tight space in your chest denied
further investigation, the last page. You swam,
your eyes stinging too freely to look back,
the frog-kicks of your legs making their own ripples.
You stood a wet mess on the slippery surface,
your body newly yours, and laughing children
emerging from the dawn around you
to jump again and again
without a second thought.

Dolphins

He lays her down as if she were
the seventh girl that day,
then grows more urgent.
She thinks that this part is the truth.

They move like his boat,
like two boats

that fight in a crowded ocean
over the right to discover the flat grey
heads of dolphins

before the animals take fright at sudden knowledge
         – the motor, the graceless movements,
the ugly unsuitable visitors –

and dip their heads
and move away, struck by the too-strong contrast
of shadows sharp against the sea.

And he peels himself off the sheet
and she off the other side.

Declaration

The ghost orchid is pale enough
to startle a squirrel, a hare,
pale enough to frazzle someone
who believes in ghosts.

The ghost orchid seizes up
under the pressure of its rareness
like a small child forced to play the violin for guests,
which she knows she does badly.
It's bad at being seen, and bad at hiding.

The ghost orchid is
the branched negative of the detective's brain.
It lies over under through beyond behind the woods
where the detective first tested an acorn
with his tongue, aged two and a half.

The ghost orchid sucks at
chlorophyll in the leaf mould
like a tired child at the breast,
thinning its petals till it's translucent
and almost given up for good.

The detective thinks
he can almost photosynthesise,
he's trying so hard. He shuffles
his feet through the rich fungus,
scuffs the earth around the orchid
in a halo, as he saves and discovers it
at the same time.

Cyclops

They found it thrown like a loosed tooth
in the abandoned corner of a scraped-out cave.
The hole like a woeful bullet in the brow
suggested monsters, something halved and mutilated.

They thought the skull
seemed bolder than an animal's,
and piled the layers on in their imaginations —
the water round the scalp, the membrane jelly,

the men's blood running through the skin,
then the hair. The archaeologist who'd always liked
to lull a man's head in her arms,
lifted it carefully when it was ready,

and heard the bones far away
in the elephant graveyards rattle, shaking
Africa and India, then hissing still;
afraid of the collapsing of the myth:

the Cyclops filtered through history
into an elephant growing smaller and smaller;
like Kumbhakarna in the Ramayana,
a giant cut down bit by bit.

Like Fish

I've been held a few times in the sea,
and know what it is to have walls of salt
bite at you as your lover does,
but even back at home I think

of fish sometimes. As we begin
our slow swim up to the round silver light
like the eye of a needle, pushing out
a space in the thick water,

I think of fish. Night-time life
is lived in lips. Your hand turns like
the passing shine of the shoal:
thousands of scales, each one touchable and precise;

turning, turning. We're blind,
our memories drawn away
so we can bump against the same landmarks
and find them new.

And there's your finger beckoning,
a hook to pull something faceless
up out of the damp. And there's you, you,
caught with a tooth on my lip;

and the underwater silence;
and the seabed rich with salt.

Absence of a Village

Like a lute's frayed metal or catgut string,
the houses have crumpled inwards
in the mountains where Orpheus first twitched.
Animals whose reason to be here is vague
come and nudge you, saying *Mule. Dog. Chicken.*

Inside the house you find white flowers. Cushions too,
and chairs, and curtains – a picture of Stalin,
crumpled against a mountain he's never seen.

On the floor, a folded piece of paper, and inside that,
another, folded, and a butterfly wing
that's a plastic flap from a leftover bottle
of ethyl, acid and essence of cherry.

Everything the way it was when they left it
for places with pavements and sewers and trash collection.
Outside, the trees are beginning to fold.

The roads seize up, the men bend at sudden angles
marking odd junctures: rickshaws, the Dover crossing,
Austrian businessmen; food queues, thrown rocks,
shades of hair found in leaf mould, women who were shot.

Scheherazade

'Age cannot wither her, nor custom stale/ Her infinite variety'
– William Shakespeare, *Antony and Cleopatra*

A story every night. Once, there was a man. *There was a man. There was a man.*
She rubs tired gems together, trying for a spark. Her black hair, perfectly
combed, is dust thrown out by lucky young dancers, the glistening of
suggestion caught in men's eyes. Her women rustle, echoes of silk in her chamber,
half-remembered. Terror grows. She follows trails like a lipsticked,

foolish dog. The words' tapestry stretches like her skin, grey, taut. He grows
old too. He closes his eyes. His stomach swells. *There was a man once. There was
a man. There was a man.* The tapestry fills with blown holes – lost nights,
nights lost – holes blown full with tapestry. *There was a man. Once there was a man.*
Swelled stomach, his eyes closed, he grows too old, skin not taut, grey hair

like stretched tapestry. Words dog foolish lipstick-like trails: followed,
terrified, half-remembered. Chamber silk echoes, rustles. Women eye men,
catch suggestions of glistening. Dance young and lucky. Thrown dust combs
hair perfectly black; her hair's sparks try together. Gems, tired,
rubbed a man. *There was a man. There was a man, once.* Every night a story.

A Private Nurse

Honouring the principle
that the honouring of life
is the only principle worth pursuing,
I laid out your body, every brick and slate
pulled from the bloody mess of guts
dappled with light. I worked to lengthen
the line of days allotted, climbed

the rich scaffolding of your solid life,

I worked like a nun, tucked back
my habit so as to see you better, well
enough to disappear into detail:
chalk falling from a pillar; the golden hinge
at one extreme of life; the burning candle
at the imperceptible, endlessly
removable end.

Blood Ties

We're sitting in the crocodile-farm restaurant
eating crocodile steak from a long glass table
while the crocodiles circle hopefully below us,

and I wonder how they kill them. Stun gun? Brave diver
with a knife, vets jostling for a bullet to the head?
Whichever, there's no guilt in handbags, shoes, suitcases

made from these, when each one flayed
drives down the value of her wild cousins' skin.
Not unlike the siblings born in labs for harvesting,

whose anxious parents stand behind thick glass
to watch the precious marrow pump through living,
dispensable bones. You take a bite of steak,

and say that when you die, you want to be fed
to the crocodiles. Someone else around the table
declares her wish to be cremated, and her ashes

to be thrown then to the North wind, the fire stripping her
of all unnecessary padding. Her way of saying
to the vast savage green world, *I was only ever*

a visitor here, I am a creature not of earth but air.

Newborn

You twitched on top of me, a god
I did not know how to handle.
My first fear, my first love. Each beat
of my heart was a new wave of light
across your brain's blank, starting screen.
Six breaths to every one of mine,
and every inch of my worn skin
felt by you like paper's gasp at ink.

Bones

First gift: the possession
of those white, amazing bones,
your little life

not touched, quiet, amassing
motion. Second gift,

a human light on them:
the ardent bites in them clack

like waking eyelids
rise to the edges,

leaving you hollow, little one;
loved.

Leaving, 1950

The big grey river
cuts through black mountains
pouring water from one hand to another.

Black, orange and blue
dragonflies clap their wings for it,
like the pale sisters thousands of miles away,

circling Scottish thorns and human emotions,
smoothing velvet sweets
down their caramel throats

as the water shushes stones as smooth
and black as olives. My grandfather investigates
the falling rock steps

discovers only stern rock doors.
In town he watches the fat crab buses
scuttle across the sand,

their grasping windows
pointing out squares
of white north light.

That Country

Dry atoms of dust scrape its surface,
small and hot. I imagine them as orange.
I imagine the hair on our arms bleached by the sun.

I'm told of its many gifts. Their names are words
outlining shapes I can't see solidly. Elephant.
Grasses. Kolkata. All that wrote your moving mouth.

I want to ask it a question, see it stop and turn
towards me like the fat earth's tilting ball. It is not quick,
or jealous. It would resent nothing I did to it.
We'll walk there and I'll paint you over, clean as air.

I'll take a mirror, take a pencil, take iced water.
We'll drift like broken parts of continents,
so slowly that our flight will be measureless.

The quick months pass. The stones fall.
Now we are leaving London, we are leaving
Paris. We are leaving Fife, Grimsby and Middlesex,
Swindon and Hendon, Keymer and Weardale,

a flood of people leaving. I count the days,
and buy an orange tent. At night all the people I've known
move forwards like growing plants over the landscape,
their delicate, complex lives spreading out to cover it.

Toothlessness

Perhaps the breast was disappeared too quickly,
anyway, I stayed orally fixated, my fingers never
out of my mouth. Each tooth was touched a hundred times a day:
sprung soldiers, each one weak. I had dreams I'd lose my teeth.

Tar beasties, sucked down, swirled inside my mouth's
rough darkness, harsh as orange peel. I dreamed of a kiss
so vast that we'd fuse like fish, enter the prehistory of kisses,
tongues larger than night or water... My husband,

we grew to be elderly. Each yellow peg fell
into our shared sink, the blood palpable taste, moist time.
Now, wet as pulp or bog, the tongue lives alone – save you –
pressing down sometimes in the darkness beneath my touch.

Still alive, my mouth. Sometimes I think I hear it moan.

My Audience Your Audience

We couldn't stop talking when we met, could only shut
each other up with bed, the narrow tank making us soundless

as fish or astronauts, but the next morning all our good work
was undone, there was more to say. The next silence

was when we saw somebody fall, and the screech of cars
span in rings away from what our ears could hear —

afterwards, though, we screamed then talked some more.
Each happening, for us, the hush of tragedy before the curtain

falls, before the rage of clapping starts, affirming, *yes, yes,*
we are between the silences, we are together now, still talking.

Lot's Wife

As she balls up hands
of crunched falafel and she sips
the sweet tea she used to scrunch her face up at,

and as she strokes
black hair on the chests of men
who look like her – as she touches them

and feels sand beneath their skin,
and reads the books her own face features in;
or rises from the big tank, clean and dripping

scented moisture like jungle rain,
even as she does these things, she knows
that once you've left a place

you can't return; that once you've left your life
you can't look back, or it'll crumble
and leave you standing in the desert,

eyes salted and unsure;
heart gone nowhere, like a closed-mouth camel
swaying off into the night.

Survival of the Fittest

Imagine a gorilla forsaking
the company of female gorillas
to live with only other men;
to walk in a routine of perfect lines, hooded,
his most florid parts kept private
beneath a long brown cloak.

Imagine a dolphin swimming
a set distance back and forth,
improving, ignoring
the games the other dolphins play around her
as she aims for the goal of better time
that burns in numbers in her brain.

Imagine a parakeet breaking
out into honking tears because of the song
coming from a radio, piano, television,
though he doesn't even know the name
of the bird singing. Not a mate or mother.

Imagine a puppy squatting
before a mirror; tilting her head, turning it;
her mouth pursed and thoughtful,
checking her own familiar face,
checking it's still familiar.

How Many Camels Is Too Many?

The soldiers pluck the air
from their mouths with cigarettes,
exhale the waste like camels:
fantastic stripes of desert on desert.

The situation's getting urgent.
They're stuck with thirty camels
between twenty-something soldiers.
No orders or instructions coming in from anywhere.

What's to be done with them —
the entrance points, the fourlegged possibilities
vanishing from the true world
like their own hoofprints in the sand?

The contents of the smugglebags
are packed up and sent away in jeeps,
the riders in their borderless clothes
the same; plus chains and warrant notes.

The camels roam around like dogs
across a landscape narrow and dumb
as a camel's eye: opiates sunk into the hairless skin
where fat is stored, glee surely hidden

just behind the curled lips.
Left absurd, and it's not their fault —
abandoned like fruit pips
spat out from cracked lips together with

not enough water. One man sits down
with his knees apart, and stares out
at the camels approaching,
at the unbelievable camels approaching.

Time Shuffle with Susie Q.

How does it happen? It begins with a tune,
and the turn of a heel, heel, as little Susie Q.
appears with a step that'll reach her obituary
long after she's married and turned conservative,

long after Lil Hardin implodes at her piano.
You shuffle a glass
on the bar, bar, and think of the others,
hip hop and a girl like this one but shinier,

who you'll take by the hips, hips,
and not bother with the steps.
Because you, you're from the future
and you can see past this neighbour/hood/ghetto,

already done the minuet, allemande and the mazurka – now the turn
of Susie's heel is neat as a twist of lime, lime,
the dip and rise hot as another girl's waist – hot as your finger

dipped in rum and held damp, damp to the pulse of an era
as Susie advances, offers / fades, answers...?

You're caught off-guard. Her double-take hits you
like a blow to the knees. And as you fall like a jitterbug, tumble,
time traveller, you've already tasted it:
the second, the shining minute

when just the right number of people knew it,
and you were one of them, and Susie the other.

Hackney

Without sun, without money, with a park, within concrete.
With stray cats, with an Oyster card, with great unpaid opportunities.
With books, with lentils, with luxury redevelopments.
With soap, without shower gel, with broadband, without experience.
With two-for-one wine, without an interview jacket.
With a £1 sack of onions, without a student card or phone credit.
Without a bike, with unmatched earrings, without dentists, without pubs.
With cigarettes, always. With big sofas, with communal mugs.
With blankets, without a watch, within a walk to the shops.
With tea, with insomnia, with borrowed spliff, with a laptop.

Noli Me Tangere

The emperor
is the man with the animals. They are
the possessions of the emperor,
it's always been like that.

Each has a very specific use.
He lifts small, expensive dogs in the mornings
to test the clout of the imperial muscle;
shirtless, while the lion's head on the wall watches him
and decides not to tell anyone

how at night, before the emperor sleeps,
he rubs his face in handfuls of mane
like a loofah buffing skin,

calms his breath according to
the vibration in the fur.

Before dinner the First Lady puts her head
through the loop of an ostrich's neck,
and the emperor smiles.

When he drives through the streets
the camels bumping the carriage
look over their shoulders with the dark, backhanded eyes
of girls in pornographic films.

It takes a while for those around him to realise
till it hits them like the last piece of clothing
dropped to the ground.
The emperor is so proud of his animals.

But there are no animals, the rumour goes,
these are something else!

The streets ring hollow,
a shiver runs through the First Lady's ostrich feathers.

The animals stir, finally
begin to ask each other,

Who do you belong to?

Llama is Watching

The best time to be alone is early morning, and the best place
a mountain, so it didn't surprise me
much
                                        when she emerged
like a cicada   into the orange dawn

        a time when usually
only the cooks are up

the mules' whinny
the pampas grass rustling under the wind's soft tread
                                        the whimsies of clouds
pulling their own shapes out of the sky
and the thick dark eyes of the herd,   their creaking canvas bags.

The trek so far had left them sick and

gasping for release –

the ability to vomit,
        space in their throats,
                a lower, deeper air
                                        but today she emerged

clean
from her tent, I heard
the rip of the thick blue zip. She was looking for a place to urinate, to unbutton

        her blue jeans and squat down, a little
hollow perhaps in the rock.
                Also for fresh water
to brush her teeth, she wanted   the taste of mint
to echo in her mouth   until the meat came.

What did surprise me was the singing goddess muffled
in six layers and then cloud.   She was so – transparent –
breath full of joy

at air, at being safe but skinless
in the middle of the toppling thin sun,
a song I know well.

                                         She spat chewed coca leaves
down to graze the living ground,

she walked
                  in hiking boots with yellow laces,
                  I half-expected

              her to bark like a triumphant dog. She stopped me in my tracks,
                  I was halfway through the chaser's turn at tig

when her bright countenance turned on me,   considered me

– her flushed cheeks froze
                  my suddenly   foolish face.

Printing Press

Thank God for the printing press, she said,
before paper it would take a flock of sheep
to make a Bible.

I see them galloping, scrubbed clean,
their warm skin taut over Genesis, Exodus,
the Nativity – blue skies and green fields
waiting for trees.

Four Self-Portraits

i – clay

Who knew that three burning months
would turn me to the sea? Who knew that fingers
thin as reeds could fill me, make a difference
to voice, touch, the pale sound
of a heart?

Cold mist flies over my beached hair,
whipped like thorns by sticks,
laughing like a child, the one
that I'd forgotten, the one with all his baby teeth in.

Sometimes I look now
at sound.

Sometimes in my bed the echoes roar,
sometimes the flat palm whispers.
Cheek to cheek, my pillow, and I,
sail.

ii – light

Never has there been a fairer place than this.
Never has hay called horses with such voracity
as I put into finding you. Never was greater care taken.

Such an animal – magnificent in light –
is only found with careful endeavour:
light as a sewing stitch, heavy as the pig we saw
abandoned on a mountain.

This is a self-portrait wrought in light. This is the right way taken.

I spin with great care, the negative
in white, white, white spread through me like a Christ,
thinner than the bare fuzz
that rises from ripe paper.

iii – wine

The lesser way is sometimes right. The heaped duvet
full of wine, your broken lips
full of wine. Today I see how the brown in a winebottle

rings around its holy cylinder.
Once I breathed inside a room, a serpent
cutting through pieces of lives left there.

Once we fell together, legs out
like geometry, bodies tight like eels.

If a cut – the hiss of red, then brown – is the worst thing to happen to you,

be lucky. Breathe lucky in the air like hope or gold,
lucky like a field of rapeseed sending out luck in circles,
the impossible dust filling the air.

iv – flame

Remember the mound burning tight against you
in the single bed; a mound burning
like a bulb, like a lamp.

Yes.

Smile for the heat of another country,
smile like reeds or cane stalks loosening
into fibres when they burn.

If I could draw a woman,
I'd paint fire.
If I could shake off the mosquitoes,
the grass-stems in the air, what would be left?

The face in a cave, uncarved, cold.
That hot body mass,
fire.

Qualia

Look into the great surge of yellow,
the unknown, sacred yellow:
a few shades lighter than the bold Egyptian colour
swept across goddess friezes up to the Near East,
a few shades darker than the noontime sky
moving into its grand point of light.

Feel the power
of that word, *yellow,* how it was sounded
by the first humans' soft lips and their softly amazed tongues.
Watch it wash across the shore, changing itself
with each wave lashed onto plain, variable beaches.
Yellow can be anything you want it to be.
Yellow describes itself. Take any word you choose.

Marguerite

Effeuiller la marguerite. Strip off the florets
like sessile hairs swelling bulbous roots
under the scalp and coming out in handfuls.

The strong yellow sphere is breathing for you
through millions of hidden nostrils.

From every direction, they tell bees what to do,
effeuille-moi, love me or love me not.

My parents looked over the ocean
and turned great-grandmother Daisy into me, Marguerite.
Marguerites grow in our garden – the dog-daisy,
the ox-eye, the moon – junky and mixed
as new words in a child's mouth.

Let me unfold you,
let me tear you down from the wall like a creeper,
its thin shoots spreading like a wealth of Catholic children.

The flower grows so vulgar,
its names shift through the past remembered
as peeled-off petals, a weighted burst of pollen.

The Space, The Calf

Whether I'm in Cambridge or Iceland or dead, the cow will be there.
– EM Forster, *The Longest Journey*

The moon's a rumour in the act of leaving
as I walk the net of fields strung along the river,
past squirrels and goslings just learning the bricks.

'The cow is there,' said Ansell. No one spoke.
The first calf for years, brick white, placed perfectly,
– the eighteenth-century calf – stands carefully

to tug with blunt teeth on the cream-coloured sky.
Bred, like the other cows, to match that square
white building opposite: his cobbled back,

that tall brick front. The river water flows so flat,
the bridges gleam against the sunlight twice:
once flesh, once detailed reflection.

Count backwards along the river's backbone:
six months since the calf was born, three years
since I arrived, three centuries since the thick white bricks

were carried into town. *One might do worse
than follow Tilliard, and suppose the cow
not to be there unless oneself was there to see her.*

How much are we allowed? Legend has it,
first-class scholars earn the right to graze
a cow or goat or sheep in this particular meadow –

beside the bridge where, legend has it,
two people can still duel with swords or guns
until one of them dies. *So familiar, so solid,*

*surely the truths she illustrated would in time
become familiar and solid also.* The heavy bellies
of the bell-towers swing into morning

with a circular sound. A few fields over,
a car-park revs up, charged with light.
I wait for day to start. The cows wait for the calf

to grow a stomach pendulous as theirs,
and the round dark eyes which know their own likeness
as well as their teeth know this grass.

In the Weald

Daisies unwind their yellow circles,
spires and spheres counting out the hours
the country mice are killing, after school.

We've stashed the bottles of wine and beer
to dampen in the trees' arm muscles
flexing below the water level,

their labels shivering verbal echoes
beneath the double view of glass and water.
Once a sheep died in this river,

her four feet in the air. Now the fields
with their continuing animal life
stretch out before us. We watch the bone-white sky,

the frogs, each other; the boys joke, drink, wrestle
on blunted throats of flattened grass.
No deadlines yet and no reason,

when we turned as a pack and ran
against the pale wheat, our t shirts and bikini tops
the purest colours in fields of change and shade.

No time to watch rain creeping over the bottles,
the sky, the river, the corpse of the forgotten sheep,
and our feet, running away from the woods.

Yellow Rattle, Vased

i.

Pick it from its cage of nettles,
doing nothing in the meadow.
Swat it from the angel-hair,
common bent and interfering cattle.

Feel the burns in your fingers crackle
as the land tells you it's not forgotten
with its own names for its parts:
hay, worm-grass, mouse-ear, caddick.

Snap it off at lowest point of stem,
your triangular hand a beak to a plant
as bright as a bird's eye;
note the bulbous yellow petals,

dappled with the orange dottles
printed on them like a psalm.
Do this on a day when you look over the field
and see nothing, not even yourself, reflected.

ii.

Bring it back with you and settle
in your house, among the chatter.
Take it to the kitchen table
to stand thin in the old milk-bottle

you bought on purpose to seem rural.
Feel yourself just the plant's chattel –
communication to the open, cleaner inside air.
Here it can be fragile,

for the last time, uncollected,
with nothing but your path to follow,

not the orange or the yellow,
no job to test the horizon's mettle,

or to knock all your joys and hassles
from your back like the yellow pollen,
that clings like a stem to spreading leaves,

like a cow's hide to her flesh;
like the name to yellow rattle.

The day you heard your father died

You must use it now, your heart,
use the wheat and seed of it,
the ears and the crop and the beating of it.
Listen to him, your heart,
before you take a step, before you write a line.

Live through that heart, his veins, his fists.
If you can, pull him up through your throat,
take a minute to kiss and recollect
the look you got when you were first given it.

Today you and he must move just right
the way you've dreamed: always
heads up, backs long and straight, like mice in corn.

Arkadi Monastery

After the fires had stopped, art started
to paint itself again. A lick of flame
hit the cooling lines of martyrs
putting their clothes back on, virgins
resettling their smiles. Faces stared again,

reshaped in smooth bone like fallen stone.
A mass of shadow stretched out along the forest,
turning the leaves to their true colours,
as the rays of the sun unshaped the day.
Small parts of the original were seen:
the curves of a face in profile, half an arm

hanging like half a story
from your grandmother's sleeve.

Horses

I saw the new-made bridles slip
into the horses' strong horse grip

at each square corner of your size;
I saw their twitching animal eyes.

I didn't see the rush of blood
that might have heralded sainthood,

but just a belly's slow collapse
upon the sharply broken back

imploding like an emptied sack;
only the slowly blossoming patch

of wine-red blood that dyed the grass
with shadows coming up unasked:

the men or queens or gods you scorned,
the sounds your people make in war.

When gazing fast into the flame
I looked for sights that didn't change;

things that stand alone, suspended
till the seer's sight has ended.

And something bright swam into view
my half-filled memory of you —

wind whistling the way you went,
to tell the nearby slipshod tents

the shining outcome of their rage:
this final scene, your halted age

left by hoofprints in the dew
as soil sucked in the last of you.

And four horses, writing out the world,
ears numb with the things they've heard,

their aching backs and angry hooves
tattoo your skin into a proof.

They run on, ears back, vomiting
with their need to pull free again.

Egill Skallagrímsson's Lausavísur

i.

The man who ruined this pub last week, tore up the floor,
you told him, didn't you, that you were out of beer?
And that bloke who always kills it on the fruit machine,
you lied and cruelly ran him out of here.

Those women who drank down death like shots
– yes, shooting Death! – you turned them away too,
and the guy who likes the girls with thunderous thighs.
He who doesn't get his round in is no friend of mine.

All these famous drinkers are coming back for you.
Easy to track you, Bárðr, through the snow;
they'll just follow the maze of false words to your tomb
and what your fate will be then, I don't know.

ii.

Red rune run
through the root of the tree.
Red rune run
between the beasts' ears.

Drink men, drink
and guard your ale.
Drink men, drink
with the giggling girls.

Red rune run
through the root of the tree.
Red rune run
between the beasts' ears.

Drink men, drink
down the lines I've carved.
Drink men, drink
we'll see how it goes down.

Red rune run
through the root of the tree.
Red rune run
between the beasts' ears.

Drink men, drink,
cough up bleeding vowels.
Drink men, drink
and pledge your puke to verse.

iii.

I'll spray to mark this spot,
I'll get drunk when you're gone!

My beard will be wet with laughs
– and my spear wet too, by dark!

An ox can take booze better than you.
I'll ram its horn through your gut to show!

Cower in my showers of victory,
your pale spirit running from Ólvi and me!

Kneeling

but it was such a small thing

        but it was such a small thing
        how could they know?

        the trickle the glisten
    of oil and sweat on our shared features
    the heavy curl of his toes when I touched them
    like a baby's fist

        and how I noticed the black hair on them
    like the hair at the meet of his collarbones

yes I thought it
    yes I imagined lingering
        perhaps I did linger – just my fingertips on the anklebone
and then I felt his eyes on me

    and then the air between us,

and knew it –

This would be my important thing!

        not the grain
    I flaked and seized

not the goats
I took by the horns.

Not the words rushing past my ears like wind,

        this would be Mary
        the only most important Mary,

me and me and me and the light.

Degas in New Orleans

The bayou is not like the Seine. It is wetter.
And the hot light is too much to paint by.
The pastry folds, the beef dries, the kitchen smells sharp.

There are no Jews that I can see
but the blacks fill the streets like steam.
This place is solid shapes trying to find each other.

The whores' fingers and toes are not correct,
and they laugh instead of smiling.
These people carry candles to funerals

and live in white rooms full of plants.
For miles there is nothing but cotton.
The churches are not tall but the sky is.

India At Last And Then

Whether you're watching stags from your back garden
beneath a stubborn Highland rainbow,

the earth firmly green, your arms a shifting beige,
or light-headed before a shrine full of light,

or feeling red wine's glow rush forwards to your jaw;
walking London's blue-grey streets in solid shoes

or signing your name in crooked ink – clothed
or naked, left or leaving, the one black god is here:

you, nineteen and not quite believing your luck,
falling back onto a bed of purple heather,

an orange sheet settling over your body
with a breath as hot, as light as women's hair.

The Bull

In truth the bull drove himself
into the doctor's office, full of rage
and heading towards anything white.
But I approved, and came at once,
and I did love that bull.

He was powerful but blind,
so when she shone her flashlight
into his dark, dumb eyes, he didn't flicker.
A tap on the knee though made him quiver,
and he beat his paws, hooves, hands;

they fell like hollow reeds to the floor;
blind rage that sounded like the pause
in the mouth before noise, rage, tears.

I tried to work with him. I rubbed him up
the wrong way, reversing the hairs on his coat
the way a careless child might corrupt
a velvet cushion. The doctor pursed her lips,

painted the room white. The bull couldn't weep,
couldn't shout; he was only a bull.
I sat down obediently
in a small green chair and crossed my legs,
talked for an hour in monochrome.

Saving for a Rainy Day

You can't plan in the Antarctic. You can't buckle straps
to your hips like a mountaineer and trek across the glass river
knowing for sure that the reflections of your feet are following.
The rain opens and closes quickly as a shower head.

Thick snow might touch your tongue before it can tap out
the words you've decided on. The clothes you put on
are ludicrous in an hour: the Shetland jumper, wetsuit, khakis,

whatever people wear. You can't ever bang the door of the igloo
and run outside because you're tired of your husband,
and expect the same door to be there when you get back.

No picnics are ever held in the Antarctic,
even on days that look sunny from the inside,
even on days when the foxes and the seals are dancing in the light,
even when you believe with all your heart that the sun will last.

Alum Bay

You dug me out
from the crust around the last man's mouth,
the scabbed blood on his lips,

scraped burnt flakes of my skin
from his bedroom walls:
the coat of spontaneous combustion.

You sieved the salt like fool's gold
from the tears I washed him in;
showed it to me, mine;

pressed all the dust together,
trying to make a shape, a sandcastle,
anything that wouldn't crumble

in your arms. Finally you poured
the long flecked stream of me into
this new life, new and narrow as glass,

tense as a bottle on a shelf.

Adapt

for Viviane

Not on the boat, not on the train,
nor signing the mortgage for your first property,
nor in the polling booths nor smelling what your skin's become:
baking powder and Woolworths' perfume,
not a salty, drifting beach...

Not throwing out 'Goodmorningd'yethinkitlookslikerain?'
in the shops or calling 'Hiyeh!' to your friends – no, she told me,
you know you've arrived when you dream in your new tongue,
your sleep full of Yorkshire puddings, coal-fumes;
brick houses, shoulderpads, sleet.

For Laurence

I used to believe in fairies
the delicate bones the skin
pure and thick as milk,
the hair that smelt of milk.

You're stopping me
from believing in fairies.
Your scars your muscles,
the hair itching across your body.

Less and less I can see
the transparent part of you.

It was a delicate thing that faith
a delicate and ferocious thing
like a child.

Soon I won't be able to see them
dancing vague across the garden
even if I try very hard.
I will have grown up.

Soon I'll be able to see you
in clear focus and real
real as the self I used to be
the person who believed in fairies.

Bonfire Night

Shot sequins of fireworks falling to the ground,
meet whispers coming up in light pollution,
and we two stand on the grass, watching
bonfires float before us, upside down.

Visible light settles like feathers on buildings,
burning their edges: bright earth filling air, a fire god rising.
You tell me about Shiva, but these days light
is nothing to hold in awe. Just a shield cutting through

the tame smoke of metal, plastic; endless, boring bombs.
The last chords drift up smiling in purple and gold.
Dark pauses like a surgeon, hand poised like a baton
over connected bones.

The Croak

She'd always kept herself aloof. Always supposed
that for a sensible woman life could be lived
sleeping with sheets instead of duvets,
never really sinking into a bath,

nibbling flakes of pastry from her pasties,
clapping politely, with fingertips only,
staying inside during heatwaves.

So it took her by surprise when at the end
– when death's grass-blade fingers
began to stroke her ribs – the lost purple frog
burst forth, choking, in her throat.

Somebody Else's Husband

If you don't get him first, somebody else will, and you'll have to spend the rest of your life knowing that somebody else is married to your husband.
– When Harry Met Sally

I caught him off guard. He was on his way
to meet that mystical couple who'd go down
in history as he'd tell it to his grandkids
sitting in tight imaginative circles

around the hearth. We each appeared
on the clear flame of the desert,
its wings burnt black like soot as it caressed
the prickly plants, the hermits, the squirming

big-eared mice. He looked surprised to see me,
till we settled into talk. We swapped jokes
and looks for months. Our souls were the same –
even the parts we lied about to each other.

I was so happy: my hair loose like a girl's,
my eyes clear as a chick's or cub's.
I kept one hand on his stomach
and the other on the sand. He kept his staff

stretched across the entrance to the cave.
Which one of us, in fact, was young?
The details were hard to find; harder to remember,
now. Perhaps I should have seen something

in the odd way he swung one foot,
or in his eyes, the bloodstained tunnel
going on and on. Now the road,
grey, heavy, goes on and on in mine.

My heart rises and sets with the sun
as I wait listlessly for travellers to appear
across the slim mouth of the horizon.

Notes

'Recapitulation Theory'
The theory of recapitulation posits that human development from embryo to adult reflects the stages of evolution.

'Song of Zagreus'
Zagreus is a variant of the Dionysos cult – specifically, a child of Zeus often clad in goatskins, who was torn apart by jealous Titans. Ancient Greeks commemorated him with secret rituals possibly including wine-drinking, orgies, and human sacrifice/cannibalism.

'Cyclops'
In prehistoric times, a form of dwarf elephant evolved on the islands of Crete, Cyprus and Sicily. The legend of the Cyclops is thought to originate with the discovery of dwarf elephant skulls. Kumbhakarna is a brother of Ravana in Hindu legend: a sleeping giant woken to fight against the hero Rama, who slowly chopped him to death.

'How Many Camels Is Too Many?'
Israeli soldiers ran into problems in dealing with Bedouin drug dealers smuggling heroin into the country, when they realised they had no guidance on what to do with the camels used to transport the drugs.

'Time Shuffle with Susie Q.'
Lillian Hardin, composer of 'Doin' the Susie-Q' – the song that popularised the well-known dance move – died while performing at a televised memorial concert for her former husband Louis Armstrong. The dance move was named for Susie-Jane Quealy (later Dwyer).

'Marguerite'
A 'marguerite' is a daisy in French and a larger form of daisy in English. *Effeuiler* is a verb describing the 'he loves me, he loves me not' game played with daisies in France and the UK. The phrase 'a wealth of Catholic children' refers to my mother's parents' large Catholic families.

'Yellow Rattle, Vased'
Yellow rattle, also known as cockscomb, is a British wildflower flowering between June and September. It is commonly used to suppress grass growth to promote greater biodiversity in hay meadows.

'Arkadi Monastery'
In 1866, Ottoman forces controlling Crete herded 900 Greek Christian women and children into the Arkadi monastery, where they blew themselves up in a mass suicide. The monastery and its artworks have now been partially restored.

'Horses'
Dismemberment by four horses was a form of capital punishment practised across Europe and Asia in the medieval and early modern periods.

'Egill Skallagrímsson's Lausavísur'
This poem is loosely based on verses, or *lausavísur,* by a tenth-century Icelandic poet called Egill Skallagrímsson. They focus on an event when Egill and his companion Ólvi are 'guests' of a man named Bárðr, who pretends to have no beer to offer them. When he's found out, the three enter into a drinking bout culminating in Bárðr's slaying by Egill and Ólvi.

'Alum Bay'
Alum Bay is a spot on the Isle of Wight near the 'Needles' multi-coloured sand and clay cliffs. Sand from the cliffs is sold here, layered in glass vials, bottles or pictures.

'Bonfire Night'
Shiva, the Hindu god known as the 'Transformer' or 'Destroyer,' is commonly portrayed smeared with ashes.

'Somebody Else's Husband'
Oedipus, who went on to kill his father and marry his mother, first gained fame by defeating the riddling Sphinx, who has the body of a lion, the wings of an eagle, and the head of a woman.

Acknowledgements

Some of the poems in this collection first appeared in the following publications: *iota, Mercy, Cadaverine, Literateur, nthposition, Rialto, Horizon Review, Asking a Shadow to Dance* (Oxfam), *Poetry South East 2010* (New Writing South), *Best British Poetry 2011* (Salt), *Salt Book of Younger Poets* (Salt), *Lung Jazz* (Eyewear) and the pamphlet *How Many Camels Is Too Many* (Holdfire).

Grateful acknowledgement is hereby made to the editors.

'I Have My Mother's Eyes' won third prize in the Café Writers Norwich Open Poetry Competition. 'Marguerite' was commissioned by Clare Whistler for the City of London festival project 'Wildflowers in City Churchyards', and 'Yellow Rattle, Vased' for the Bunces Barn project. The first part of 'Egill Skallagrímsson's Lausavísur' was commissioned for *Modern Poets on Viking Poetry*, published by the University of Cambridge's ASNAC department.

EYEWEAR PUBLISHING